Casserole Recipes

Delicious Casserole Recipes from Around the World

TABLE OF CONTENTS

INTRODUCTION VII

A FEW TIPS: VIII

CHAPTER ONE: CLASSIC CASSEROLE RECIPES 1

CHICKEN TETRAZZINI 1

SHEPHERD'S PIE 4

CHEESY TUNA NOODLE CASSEROLE 6

INGREDIENTS: 6

BEEF, MACARONI AND TOMATO CASSEROLE 8

KING RANCH CHICKEN CASSEROLE 10

TRADITIONAL ITALIAN LASAGNA 11

FRENCH CASSOULET 14

SOUTHWESTERN TAMALE PIE 18

TATER TOT HOT DISH 20

SAUSAGE, PEPPER, AND GRITS CASSEROLE 21

MAC AND CHEESE WITH HAM AND BROCCOLI 24

CHICKEN, MUSHROOM, AND WILD RICE CASSEROLE 26

MEXICAN CHICKEN ENCHILADAS 29

SWEDISH CASSEROLE 31

GERMAN CASSEROLE 32

ZITI CHICKEN CASSEROLE 34

PORK CHOP AND POTATO CASSEROLE 35

PULLED BEEF SHEPHERD'S PIE 37

CHAPTER TWO: BREAKFAST CASSEROLE RECIPES 38

CLASSIC BREAKFAST SAUSAGE CASSEROLE 38

FARMER'S BRUNCH CASSEROLE 40

EVERYTHING BAGEL CASSEROLE 41

BRUNCH LASAGNA 43

CHICKEN 'N WAFFLES CASSEROLE 45

LOADED CAULIFLOWER BREAKFAST BAKE 46

CHEESY HASH BROWN CASSEROLE 48

BREAKFAST CASSEROLE 49

CHAPTER THREE: MEATLESS CASSEROLE RECIPES 50

CLASSIC CHEESY MUSHROOM AND BROCCOLI CASSEROLE 50

CLASSIC GREEN BEAN CASSEROLE 52

Savory Tomato Cobbler 53

Broccoli Quinoa Casserole...55

Zucchini-and-Spinach Lasagna 57

Vegan Shepherd's Pie...59

Fresh Vegetable Lasagna 61

CHAPTER FOR: SLOW COOKER CASSEROLE RECIPES................63

Cheesy Chicken Tater Tot Casserole.......................................63

Enchilada Casserole..65

Sweet Potato & Chicken Casserole 66

Taco Casserole 67

Broccoli, Brown Rice and Cheddar Casserole 69

CHAPTER FIVE: DESSERT CASSEROLE RECIPES........................71

Sweet Potato Dessert Casserole 71

Pineapple Casserole Dessert..73

Banana Pudding 74

Apple Bread Pudding with Vanilla Sauce.................................76

CONCLUSION..78

Introduction

I want to thank you for choosing this book, *Casserole Recipes: Delicious Casserole Recipes from Around the World.'*

Casseroles are the easiest way to celebrate any occasion. If you have a relative coming over or a friend visiting you and you haven't seen them for years, surprise them with a breakfast casserole and it looks like you have prepared an elaborate meal but, in reality, it is not too much work. If you were to ask someone why they always cook casseroles, you may hear answers like "because it's comfort food, easy to make, and easy to carry over for dinner at friends." But, here is the truth – a casserole is an economic investment. There is enough food for everybody to eat.

A casserole serves any occasion and is easy to put together. All you need are a few ingredients, a baking pan and an oven. There are not many dishes that can give you all the satisfaction that you want. You may be craving for a classic casserole or an inventive casserole with a twist. Either way, the collection of recipes in this book will satisfy your cravings with minimal effort, cleanup and time!

The recipes in this book can serve as breakfast, meatless, classic casseroles and desserts depending on your liking. All you need to do is whip up one of these recipes over the weekend and split the casserole to serve as a meal over the week. If you have had a terrible day, you could simply eat a casserole. You will find your spirits lifting within no time.

I hope you enjoy the recipes in the book. They were designed to help to make your life easier by preparing meals that are easy and quick to prepare.

A Few Tips:

1. If using noodles or pasta, follow the directions on the package but keep it undercooked. Drain it a couple of minutes before al dente.

2. While using meat, after browning meat, drain the fat remaining in the pan unless mentioned otherwise.

3. Frozen vegetables need not be thawed.

4. Once out of the oven, let the casserole sit for a few minutes.

5. In case you make your casserole in advance, cover and refrigerate it, remove from the refrigerator at least 30 minutes before baking.

6. Leftovers can be stored in an airtight container and refrigerated or frozen. To use, thaw completely and reheat in the oven or microwave.

7. It is advisable to place a baking tray below the casserole dish to catch any overflow of ingredients while it is baking.

Chapter One

Classic Casserole Recipes

Chicken Tetrazzini

Serves: 8-10

Ingredients:

- 1 medium head cauliflower
- 1 cup butter
- 8 cloves garlic, peeled, sliced
- 6-8 cups shredded chicken breast
- 16 ounces mushrooms, sliced
- 6 tablespoons flour
- 1 cup dry sherry
- 2 cups shallots or onions, chopped
- Salt to taste
- A large pinch freshly ground nutmeg

- Freshly ground pepper to taste

- 4 cups chicken broth or stock

- 2 cups parmesan cheese, grated

- 2 cups heavy cream

- 16 ounces extra wide egg noodles

- 2 cups panko bread crumbs

- ½ cup fresh flat leaf parsley, chopped

Method:

1. Place a pot with 3-4 cups water over medium heat. Add the cauliflower and cover with a lid.

2. Cook for 7-8 minutes or until tender. Drain and chop the cauliflower into florets.

3. Cook noodles following the directions on the package.

4. Place a large skillet over medium heat. Add ½ cup butter. When butter melts, add mushroom and sauté until tender.

5. Stir in garlic and shallots and sauté for 2-3 minutes.

6. Stir in the flour and stir constantly for a minute.

7. Pour sherry. Stir constantly. Scrape the bottom of the pan to remove any browned bits that may be stuck.

8. Add chicken stock and stir constantly. Bring to the boil.

9. Lower heat and simmer for 5 minutes. Add heavy cream, salt, pepper and nutmeg. Turn off the heat.

10. Add cauliflower, noodles and chicken into the sauce and mix well. Spoon into a casserole dish.

11. Melt remaining butter and pour over the panko breadcrumbs. Toss well. Sprinkle Parmesan cheese and toss well.

12. Sprinkle the breadcrumbs on top of the chicken mixture. At this stage, you can cover the dish with plastic wrap and refrigerate until use.

13. Bake in a preheated oven at 350°F for 30-45 minutes or golden brown on top.

14. Garnish with parsley and serve.

Shepherd's Pie

Serves:

Ingredients:

- 22 ½ ounces refrigerated cooked beef roast au jus (from the package), cut into ½ inch cubes, discard au jus

- 4 ½ tablespoons all-purpose flour

- 1 ½ teaspoon dried fines herbs, crushed

- 1 ½ cups frozen pearl onions

- Pepper powder to taste

- 3 tablespoons butter, melted

- ½ cup butter

- 1 ½ cups milk

- 1 ½ packages (10 ounces each) frozen mixed vegetables

- ¾ cup rose or beef broth

- 4 ½ cups prepared mashed potatoes

Method:

1. Place a large saucepan over medium heat. Add butter. When butter melts, add flour and sauté for 15-20 seconds.

2. Pour milk and stir constantly. Add fines herbs and stir. In a while, the sauce will thicken.

3. Add meat, onions, vegetables, rose broth and pepper and stir. Cook for a couple of minutes. Turn off the heat.

4. Transfer into a baking dish or casserole dish. Spread it evenly.

5. Spread the mashed potatoes evenly over it. Drizzle the melted butter over the mashed potatoes.

6. Bake in a preheated oven at 350°F for 30-45 minutes or golden brown on top.

Cheesy Tuna Noodle Casserole

Serves: 12

Ingredients:

- 2 cans (12 ounces each) chunk white tuna in water, drained
- ½ cup butter
- 2 tablespoons butter, melted
- 2 cups celery, chopped
- 2 cups red sweet pepper, chopped
- ½ cup onions, chopped
- 2 cups cheddar cheese, cubed
- 2/3 cup chicken broth
- 1 cup panko bread crumbs
- 4 ½ cups milk
- 6 cups wide, dried egg noodles
- 2 tablespoons dried parsley flakes or 4 tablespoons fresh parsley, chopped
- Salt to taste
- Pepper to taste
- 3-4 tablespoons Dijon style mustard
- ½ cup parmesan cheese, freshly grated

Method:

1. Grease a large rectangular baking dish or 2 smaller baking dishes with a little oil or butter and set aside.

2. Cook noodles following the directions on the package.

3. Place a saucepan over medium heat. Add butter. When butter melts, add sweet pepper, onion and celery and sauté until tender. Stir occasionally.

4. Add flour, salt, pepper and mustard and mix well.

5. Pour milk and stir constantly until it thickens slightly. Turn off heat.

6. Pour into the pot of noodles. Add tuna and cheddar cheese and fold gently.

7. Spoon the mixture into the baking dish.

8. Mix together in a bowl, panko breadcrumbs, parsley and Parmesan cheese. Add melted butter and stir until well combined.

9. Sprinkle over the tuna mixture. At this stage, you can cover the dish with plastic wrap and refrigerate until use.

10. Bake in a preheated oven at 350°F for 30-45 minutes or golden brown on top.

Beef, Macaroni and Tomato Casserole

Serves: 6-8

Ingredients:

- 1 ½ pounds ground beef
- 1 ½ teaspoons dried basil
- 1 ½ teaspoons dried oregano
- 10 cloves garlic, minced
- 1 large onion, chopped
- Pepper to taste
- Salt to taste
- 1 large green bell pepper, chopped
- 1 ½ cans (14 ounces each) canned diced tomatoes, with its liquid
- 12 ounces elbow macaroni or bow tie pasta
- 1/3 cup parmesan cheese
- 12 ounces mozzarella cheese, shredded
- 1 ½ cans (8 ounces each) canned tomato sauce

Method:

1. Cook macaroni following the directions on the package.

2. Place a skillet over medium heat. Add beef, garlic, onion, herbs, salt and green pepper and sauté until beef is brown.

3. Stir in the tomatoes and tomato sauce and stir.

8

4. Lower heat and cook for 10 minutes. Turn off heat. Add macaroni and transfer into a greased casserole dish.

5. Sprinkle Parmesan cheese and mozzarella cheese.

6. Bake in a preheated oven at 350°F for 20-25 minutes or until bubbling.

King Ranch Chicken Casserole

Serves: 7-8

Ingredients:

- 2-2 ½ pounds chicken, into large pieces

- 1 carrot, cut into 3 pieces

- 1 rib celery, cut into 3 pieces

- ½ teaspoon salt

- 1 small green bell pepper, chopped

- 1 small onion, chopped

- ½ can (from a 10.75 ounce can) cream of chicken soup

- ½ can (from a 10.75 ounces can) cream of mushroom soup

- ½ teaspoon ground cumin

- 1 ½ cups sharp cheddar cheese, grated

- 6 fajita size corn tortillas (6 inches each) cut into ½ inch strips

- 1 tablespoon butter

- ½ teaspoons salt

- ½ teaspoon dried oregano

- ½ teaspoon Mexican style chili powder

Method:

1. Place a Dutch oven over medium high heat. Add chicken, carrot, celery and salt and pour enough water to cover the chicken.

2. When it begins to boil, lower heat and cover with a lid. Simmer until chicken is tender. Turn off the heat.

3. Remove chicken with a slotted spoon and place on your cutting board. Use about 1/3 cup of broth and use the remaining broth in some other recipe.

4. Meanwhile, place a skillet over medium high heat. Add butter. When butter melts, add onion and sauté until translucent. Stir in bell pepper and garlic and cook for 2-3 minutes.

5. Add 1/3-cup broth, soups, tomatoes, oregano and spices and stir. Simmer for 5-6 minutes. Stir occasionally.

6. Shred the chicken into bite size pieces.

7. Grease a casserole dish with a little oil or butter.

8. Place half the chicken in the dish.

9. Spread half the soup mixture followed by ½ cup cheese. Spread half the tortilla strips.

10. Repeat the above 2 steps. Finally, sprinkle remaining cheese on top.

11. Bake in a preheated oven at 350°F for 20-25 minutes or until bubbling.

Traditional Italian Lasagna

Serves: 12

Ingredients:

- 1 ½ pounds ground beef
- 3 cans (6 ounces each) tomato paste
- 4 ½ cans (8 ounces each) tomato sauce
- 18 ounces bulk pork sausage
- 3 cloves garlic, minced
- 1 ½ teaspoons Italian seasoning
- Pepper to taste
- Salt to taste
- 5 medium eggs
- 3 teaspoons sugar
- 1/3 cup fresh parsley, minced
- 12 ounces ricotta cheese
- 4 ½ cups 4% small curd cottage cheese
- ¾ cup parmesan cheese, grated
- 4 ½ cups part skim mozzarella cheese, shredded, divided
- 9 slices provolone cheese
- 13 ½ sheets lasagna noodles

Method:

1. Place a skillet over medium heat. Add beef and sausage and cook until it is not pink anymore. Break it simultaneously as it cooks.

2. Add garlic, sugar, salt, pepper, tomato sauce, tomato paste and Italian seasoning and stir.

3. Lower heat and cook for about an hour. Do not cover while cooking. Taste and adjust the seasoning if necessary. Turn off the heat.

4. Meanwhile, cook the lasagna noodles following the directions on the package.

5. Add eggs into a bowl and beat lightly. Add cottage cheese, ricotta cheese, parsley and Parmesan cheese and stir.

6. Take a large baking dish of about 15 by 12 inches and spread about 1 ½ cups meat mixture. Place 4-5 noodle sheets over it. Place 3-4 provolone cheese slices.

7. Spread 3 cups cottage cheese mixture followed by 1 ½ cups mozzarella cheese.

8. Place 3-4 noodle sheets. Layer with some meat mixture followed by remaining cottage cheese. Sprinkle 1 ½ cups mozzarella cheese.

9. Place remaining noodles followed by remaining sauce and remaining mozzarella cheese. Cover the dish with foil.

10. Bake in a preheated oven at 375°F for 50-60 minutes. Uncover and bake for 15 minutes.

French Cassoulet

Serves: 6

Ingredients:

- 6 cups chicken broth
- ½ pound garlic sausage
- ½ pound slab bacon, sliced into ¼ inch thick slices
- ¾ pound lamb shoulder or leg, boneless, cut into large cubes
- ¾ pound pork loin, boneless, cut into large cubes
- 1 ½ cups dry navy beans, soaked in water for 3-4 hours
- 1 small whole yellow onion, peeled
- 2 bouquet-garni
- Salt to taste
- Freshly ground pepper to taste
- ½ cup leeks, diced
- ½ cup parsnips, sliced
- ½ cup carrots, sliced
- ½ teaspoon garlic, minced
- 3 tablespoons olive oil
- 2 tablespoons all-purpose flour
- 3 cups beef broth
- 14 ounces duck Confit

- 3 tablespoons dry white wine

- ½ cup plum tomatoes, chopped

- ¾ cup bread crumbs

- 2 cloves garlic, peeled

- A handful fresh parsley, chopped

Method:

1. Add chicken broth into a soup pot and place the pot over high heat.

2. When it begins to boil, add beans and bacon and lower the heat.

3. Cover and cook until beans are tender. If you have a pressure cooker or instant pot, you can cook the beans in it. It is much faster. Add salt and simmer for another 15-20 minutes. Turn off the heat.

4. Stir in 1 bouquet garni, sausage, onion, garlic cloves and bacon into the pot.

5. Simmer until the sausages and bacon are cooked. Remove bouquet garni and discard it. Remove onion, garlic with a slotted spoon and discard it. Set aside the sausage and bacon.

6. Place a colander over a bowl. Strain the beans into the colander. Set aside the beans and add the cooked liquid back into the pot.

7. Let the liquid simmer until the liquid is half its original quantity. Turn off the heat and set aside the cooked liquid.

8. Sprinkle salt and pepper over lamb and pork.

9. Place a casserole dish over medium high heat. Add oil. When oil is heated, add pork and lamb and cook until golden brown on all the sides. Remove the meat and place in a bowl. Keep warm.

10. Add leeks into the casserole dish and sauté for a minute. Stir in carrots and parsnips and cook until the leeks are golden brown in color.

11. Stir in the garlic and sauté for a few seconds until fragrant.

12. Stir in the flour and stir constantly for a couple of minutes.

13. Add wine and 1 ½ cups beef broth. Stir until well combined.

14. Add tomatoes and the other bouquet garni. Mix well.

15. Add the duck Confit, lamb and pork along with the cooked juices. Add more broth if required. The meat should be covered in broth.

16. Cover the casserole. Place the dish in the oven.

17. Bake in a preheated oven at 375°F for 50-60 minutes or until the meat is tender. Skim the surface whenever necessary.

18. Discard the covering of the sausage and cut into ¼ inch thick slices.

19. Cut the bacon into ¼ inch thick pieces.

20. Remove the casserole from the oven. Place sausage and bacon over it. Spread half the beans over it.

21. Place duck Confit over it. Spread remaining beans. Pour the thickened cooked liquid that was set aside.

22. Mix together in a bowl bread crumbs and parsley and sprinkle all over the Cassoulet. Do not cover the dish.

23. Bake in a preheated oven at 300°F for a couple of hours. A crust would have formed on the top.

Southwestern Tamale Pie

Serves: 4

Ingredients:

- ½ tablespoon vegetable oil
- ½ green bell pepper, finely chopped
- 1 small onion, finely chopped
- 1 jalapeño pepper, deseeded, minced
- ¾ cup corn kernels, fresh or frozen
- 1 ½ tablespoons tomato paste
- 2 teaspoons ground cumin
- ¼ cup black olives, sliced (optional)
- 7.5 ounces canned diced tomatoes, drained
- ¾ pound ground beef
- 1 tablespoon chili powder
- 1 teaspoon kosher salt
- 2 ounces Monterey Jack cheese, shredded

For the cornbread topping:

- ¾ cup yellow cornmeal
- 1 tablespoon granulated sugar
- ½ teaspoon salt
- ½ cup whole milk
- ½ cup all-purpose flour

- ½ tablespoon baking powder

- 1 egg

- 3 tablespoons unsalted butter, melted

Method:

- Place a skillet over medium high heat. Add oil. When the oil is heated, add onion, jalapeño and bell pepper and sauté until tender. Transfer into a bowl.

- Place the pan back over medium heat. Add beef and cook until brown. Break it simultaneously as it cooks.

- Add the sautéed vegetables back into the pan. Add corn, tomato paste, tomatoes, salt and spices. Mix until well combined.

- Lower heat and simmer for 10-15 minutes. Turn off the heat. Add olives if using and stir. Transfer into a casserole dish. Spread it evenly.

- To make cornbread topping: Add cornmeal, baking powder, sugar and salt into a bowl and stir.

- Add eggs, melted butter and milk into another bowl and whisk well. Pour this mixture into the bowl of cornmeal. Mix until well combined. Do not over mix.

- Spread this over the beef mixture in the casserole. Spread it evenly.

- Bake in a preheated oven at 375°F for 30-40 minutes or until the top is golden brown. A toothpick when inserted in the center of the cornbread should come out clean.

Tater Tot Hot Dish

Serves: 4

Ingredients:

- ½ pound 80% lean ground beef

- 2 tablespoons extra-virgin olive oil

- 1 cup frozen cut green beans, thawed

- 1 can (10 ounces) cream of mushroom soup

- Salt to taste

- Freshly ground black pepper to taste

- 1 cup frozen corn kernels, thawed

- ½ pound frozen shredded potato nuggets

Method:

1. Place a skillet over medium heat. Add oil. When the oil is heated, add onions and sauté until light brown.

2. Add beef and cook until brown. Break it simultaneously as it cooks.

3. Add salt and pepper and stir. Scrape the bottom of the pan to remove any browned bits.

4. Spoon the beef mixture into a baking dish. Spread the green beans and corn over the beef.

5. Pour cream of mushroom soup all over. Place frozen potato nuggets.

6. Bake in a preheated oven at 350°F for 45-60 minutes or until the potato nuggets are golden brown.

Sausage, Pepper, and Grits Casserole

Serves: 9-10

Ingredients:

For cheesy grits topping:

- 1 ½ cups milk

- 3 cups sharp cheddar cheese, shredded

- 1 teaspoon salt or to taste

- 3 large eggs, lightly beaten

- ¾ cup quick cooking grits, uncooked

- A handful fresh thyme leaves, chopped

- Freshly ground black pepper to taste

For the sausage filling:

- 1 ½ packages (19 ounces each) mild Italian sausages

- 3 large red bell pepper, sliced

- 5 cloves garlic, peeled, minced

- 1 large red onion, sliced

- 1 ½ cans (14.5 ounces each) diced tomatoes with garlic and onions, drained

- 6 tablespoons all-purpose flour

- 2 ½ tablespoons grape jelly

- ¾ teaspoon freshly ground black pepper

- 1 ½ tablespoons canola oil

- 6 tablespoons butter

- 2 ¼ cups low sodium chicken broth

- 1 ½ teaspoons red wine vinegar

- ½ teaspoon salt

Method:

1. To make grits: Add milk and 1-½ cups of water into a large saucepan.

2. Place the saucepan over medium heat.

3. When it begins to boil, add grits and cook until thick. Stir frequently. Add pepper, cheese and thyme leaves and stir. Turn off the heat.

4. Take out about ¼ of the grits mixture and add into the bowl of eggs. Whisk well.

5. Pour the egg mixture into the saucepan and whisk until well combined.

6. To make sausage filling: Place a skillet over medium heat. Add oil. When the oil is heated, add sausage and cook until brown on all the sides.

7. Retain about 1-½ tablespoons of the fat in the skillet and discard the rest.

8. Add bell pepper and onion and sauté until tender.

9. Stir in the garlic and sauté until fragrant.

10. When the sausages are cool enough to handle, cut into ½ inch thick slices.

11. Add tomatoes, sausages and bell pepper mixture into a bowl. Toss well and set aside.

12. Place the skillet back over medium heat. Add butter. When butter melts, add flour and stir constantly until light brown.

13. Add broth and whisk until well combined. Stir constantly until it begins to boil.

14. Lower heat and simmer until thick.

15. Add jelly, vinegar, salt and pepper and mix well. Add sausage mixture and mix well.

16. Transfer into a large greased baking dish.

17. Spread the grits mixture evenly over the top.

18. Bake in a preheated oven at 375°F for 20-25 minutes or until light brown.

Mac and Cheese with Ham and Broccoli

Serves: 4

Ingredients:

- 1 small head broccoli, chopped into florets
- 2 tablespoons olive oil
- 1 clove garlic, minced
- ¾ cup milk
- 6 ounces cooked ham, chopped
- 2 tablespoons panko breadcrumbs
- 1 cup elbow macaroni
- 1 small onion, chopped
- 1 ½ tablespoons all-purpose flour
- 1 cup sharp cheddar cheese, shredded
- Salt to taste
- Pepper to taste

Method:

1. Place a sheet of aluminum foil on a baking sheet. Spray with cooking spray.

2. Spread the broccoli on the baking sheet.

3. Bake in a preheated oven at 400°F for 15-20 minutes or until broccoli is tender.

4. Cook macaroni following the directions on the package.

5. Place a skillet over medium heat. Add oil. When the oil is heated, add onions and sauté until translucent.

6. Stir in the garlic and sauté for a minute until aromatic. Add flour and sauté for a minute.

7. Add milk gradually, stirring constantly all the time. Keep stirring until the sauce is thick. Turn off the heat.

8. Add cheese, salt and pepper and stir. Add macaroni, ham and broccoli and stir.

9. Transfer into a greased casserole dish. Sprinkle breadcrumbs on top.

10. Place in a preheated oven and broil for a few minutes until the top is golden brown.

Chicken, Mushroom, and Wild Rice Casserole

Serves: 4

Ingredients:

- ¼ cup wild rice
- 1 cup water
- 1 pound chicken breasts, skinless, boneless, trimmed of fat
- 1 leek chopped
- ½ cup dry sherry
- 1 cup low fat milk
- 1 tablespoon extra-virgin olive oil
- ¾ pound mushrooms, sliced
- 2 tablespoons all-purpose flour
- ¼ cup parmesan cheese, grated
- A handful fresh flat leaf parsley
- Freshly ground pepper to taste
- Salt to taste
- 1 cup frozen French cut green beans
- ¼ cup low fat sour cream
- ¼ cup almonds, sliced

Method:

1. Add water and rice into a small heavy saucepan. Place the saucepan over high heat.

2. When water begins to boil, lower heat and cover with a lid. Simmer until it is cooked. Drain and set aside.

3. Place a skillet over medium heat. Add chicken and a little salt. Cover with water.

4. When it begins to boil, lower heat and simmer until chicken is tender. Remove chicken with a slotted spoon and place on your cutting board.

5. When cool enough to handle, cut into smaller pieces.

6. Meanwhile, place a skillet over medium heat. Add oil. When the oil is heated, add leeks and sauté until light brown.

7. Stir in the mushrooms and cook for 8-10 minutes.

8. Stir in the sherry. Raise the heat to high heat and cook until most of the sherry is evaporated.

9. Sprinkle flour over the mushrooms and toss well. Pour milk and stir constantly until it thickens.

10. Lower heat and simmer for a minute. Add sour cream, salt, pepper, Parmesan cheese and parsley. Mix well. Turn off the heat.

11. Grease a casserole dish with cooking spray. Spoon rice into the dish. Spread it evenly.

12. Place a layer of chicken followed by green beans. Spoon sauce over it and spread it evenly.

13. Top with almonds.

14. Bake in a preheated oven at 350°F for about 20-30 minutes or until almonds are golden brown.

Mexican Chicken Enchiladas

Serves: 5

Ingredients:

- 2 chicken breasts
- 5 medium flour tortillas
- 1 small onion, diced
- 1 can red enchilada sauce
- 1-2 jalapeños, chopped (optional)
- 7-8 ounces canned black beans (optional)
- 1 ½ cups cheddar cheese, shredded
- 1 cup cooked white rice (optional)

Method:

1. Place a pot of water over high heat. Add chicken and boil until the chicken is cooked through. Drain and place the chicken on your cutting board.

2. When it is cool enough to handle, shred the chicken.

3. Place the shredded chicken in a bowl. Add cheese, onion, black beans, jalapeños, rice and ½ can enchilada sauce. Mix well.

4. Divide the mixture amongst the tortillas and place the filling in each of the tortillas. Roll and place in a baking dish with its seam side facing down.

5. Pour the remaining enchilada sauce on top of the tortillas. Sprinkle cheese.

6. Bake in a preheated oven at 350°F for about 20-30 minutes.

7. Serve with a lettuce salad or beans or rice or sour cream. Serve with any or more of these serving options.

Swedish Casserole

Serves: 4

Ingredients:

- 1 large onion, cut into 5 mm wide strips
- 3 potatoes, peeled, cut into strips
- 1 tablespoon dry bread crumbs
- 7 fillets Swedish anchovies or regular anchovies
- ¾ cup thickened cream
- ½ tablespoon melted butter

Method:

1. Grease a baking dish with a little butter.

2. Place onions in the bottom of the dish. Spread it evenly.

3. Spread anchovies evenly over the onions.

4. Layer with potatoes. Pour cream on top.

5. Mix together breadcrumbs and butter in a small bowl until it is crumbly. Sprinkle breadcrumbs over the cream layer.

6. Bake in a preheated oven at 400°F for about 35-45 minutes or until the top is golden brown and the potatoes are cooked through.

German Casserole

Serves: 4-5

Ingredients:

- 2 large raw potatoes, halved, cut into ¼ inch thick slices

- 14 ounces sauerkraut

- 2 tablespoons butter, chopped

- 1 large onion, thinly sliced

- 30 ounces kielbasa or 20 ounces Polish sausage or 30 ounces smoked sausage, cut into chunks on the diagonal

- Salt to taste

- Pepper to taste

Method:

1. Grease a casserole dish that has a lid. Place butter on the bottom of the dish.

2. Layer with potatoes followed by onions.

3. Spread sauerkraut over the onions. Sprinkle salt and pepper.

4. Place sausages over it. Press it lightly so that the ingredients fit well in the dish.

5. Cover with lid.

6. Bake in a preheated oven at 400°F for about 35-45 minutes or until the top is golden brown and the potatoes are cooked through.

7. Serve with bread preferably home baked bread.

Ziti Chicken Casserole

Serves: 6-8

Ingredients:

- 3 cups ziti pasta

- 3 cups Muenster cheese

- 18 ounces canned chunk dark and white meat chicken, drained

- 1 ½ cans (10 ounces each) cream of chicken soup

- Pepper to taste

- 1 ½ soup cans water

Method:

1. Cook ziti following the directions on the package. Drain.

2. Add all the ingredients except cheese into a greased casserole dish.

3. Sprinkle Parmesan cheese.

4. Bake in a preheated oven at 350°F for about 20-30 minutes.

Pork Chop and Potato Casserole

Serves: 8

Ingredients:

- 8 pork chops (1 inch each)
- 1 large onion, halved, thinly sliced
- 6 medium potatoes, peeled, rinsed, thinly sliced
- 1 ½ cups cheddar cheese, shredded
- 1 ½ cups milk
- 1 ½ cans condensed cream of mushroom soup
- 1 teaspoon garlic powder (optional)
- 2 tablespoons parsley, chopped (optional)
- ¼ teaspoon red pepper flakes (optional)
- 1 ½ tablespoons vegetable oil

Method:

1. Place a large skillet over medium high heat. Add oil and pork. (Cook in batches if necessary) Sauté until the pork is brown. Set aside.

2. Place the potato slices and onion slices in a baking dish.

3. Place the pork over the potato layer.

4. Sprinkle red pepper flake, garlic powder and parsley over it (if using).

5. Mix together in a bowl, soup and milk and pour over the potatoes.

6. Bake in a preheated oven at 350°F for about 20-30 minutes.

7. Sprinkle cheese on top and bake for another 20-30 minutes.

Pulled Beef Shepherd's Pie

Serves: 8

Ingredients:

- 8 cups pulled beef or pulled pork
- 8 sweet potatoes, peeled, chopped
- 4 carrots, peeled, chopped
- 2 red onions, chopped
- 2 stalks celery, chopped
- Salt to taste
- Pepper to taste

Method:

1. Place sweet potatoes in a large saucepan. Cover with water. Cook until tender. Drain the water and place in a bowl.

2. Mash with a potato masher. Add salt and pepper and stir.

3. Mix together in a bowl, onions, celery and carrots.

4. Grease a few ovenproof ramekins with a little oil.

5. Place a layer of pulled beef in each of the ramekins. Layer with a little carrot onion mixture. Place mashed sweet potatoes over it.

6. Place the ramekins on a baking sheet.

7. Bake in a preheated oven at 400°F for about 35-45 minutes.

Chapter Two

Breakfast Casserole Recipes

Classic Breakfast Sausage Casserole

Serves: 8-10

Ingredients:

- 2 pounds fresh bulk pork sausage with sage

- Butter to grease

- 4 cups half and half

- 2 teaspoons salt

- 1 loaf sliced white bread, cut into 1 inch cubes

- 20 ounces sharp cheddar cheese, grated

- 2 teaspoons dry mustard

- 10 large eggs, lightly beaten

Method:

1. Grease a large casserole dish with butter. Place the bread cubes in the dish. Spread it evenly.

2. Place a large skillet over medium heat. Add sausages and cook until it is not pink anymore.

3. Remove sausages with a slotted spoon and spread it over the bread evenly.

4. Sprinkle cheese on top.

5. Add eggs, mustard, salt and half and half into a bowl and whisk well. Pour into the casserole dish. Do not stir.

6. Cover the dish with foil. Place the dish in the refrigerator for 7-8 hours.

7. Bake in a preheated oven at 350°F for about 50-60 minutes.

Farmer's Brunch Casserole

Serves: 12

Ingredients:

- 6 cups frozen hash brown potatoes
- 1 ½ cups ham, diced
- 1 ½ cups Monterey Jack cheese, shredded
- 1 ½ cups cheddar cheese, shredded
- 1/2 cup green onions, sliced
- 12 eggs, beaten or 3 cups frozen fat free liquid egg product
- 2 cans (12 ounces each) canned evaporated milk
- Salt to taste
- Pepper powder to taste
- Cooking spray

Method:

1. Spray a large baking dish with cooking spray. Spread the hash brown potatoes on the bottom of the dish.

2. Sprinkle green onions and ham. Sprinkle cheese over it.

3. Mix together in a bowl, eggs, milk, salt and pepper. Whisk well. Pour over the cheese.

4. Cover with aluminum foil.

5. Bake in a preheated oven at 350°F for about 50-60 minutes or until set.

Everything Bagel Casserole

Serves: 4-5

Ingredients:

- 2 everything bagels, chopped
- ¾ cup cherry tomatoes, halved
- 1 small red onion, thinly sliced
- 1 ¼ cups milk
- Salt to taste
- Cayenne pepper to taste
- ¾ cup Sharp white cheddar, shredded
- 4 ounces cream cheese, cut into small cubes
- 4 large eggs
- 2 green onions, thinly sliced
- Freshly ground black pepper to taste
- Cooking spray

Method:

1. Grease a small baking dish with cooking spray.

2. Spread half the bagel pieces in the dish evenly.

3. Layer with half of each of the following – cheddar cheese, tomatoes, cream cheese, and red onions, in the order mentioned.

4. Repeat the above 2 steps once more.

5. Add eggs and milk into a bowl and whisk well. Retain some green onions and add rest of it into the bowl of

eggs. Add salt, pepper and cayenne pepper and whisk well.

6. Pour over the casserole dish.

7. Cover with aluminum foil.

8. Bake in a preheated oven at 350°F for about 30-40 minutes or until set.

9. Uncover and bake until the top is golden brown.

10. Sprinkle green onions on top and serve.

Brunch Lasagna

Serves: 4-5

Ingredients:

- ½ pound frozen shredded hash browns
- 4 slices bacon
- 5 eggs
- Salt to taste
- 3 small flour tortillas
- 1 cup cheddar cheese, shredded
- ½ tablespoon butter
- 2 tablespoons heavy cram
- Freshly ground black pepper to taste
- 2 tablespoons chives, chopped
- Cooking spray

Method:

1. Spray a baking dish with cooking spray.

2. Place a skillet over medium heat. Add bacon and cook until crisp. Remove with a slotted spoon and place over layers of paper towels. When cool enough to handle, chop into pieces.

3. Do not discard the fat in the pan.

4. Add hash browns and sauté until it starts turning golden brown. Stir frequently.

5. Sprinkle salt and pepper and stir. Turn off the heat.

6. Add eggs and cream in a bowl and whisk until smooth and creamy.

7. Place a nonstick skillet over medium heat. Add butter. When butter melts, pour the egg mixture.

8. Scramble the eggs and cook until soft. Add chives, salt and pepper and stir. Turn off the heat.

9. Place a tortilla in the baking dish. Spread half the hash browns over the tortilla followed by half the eggs, 1/3 the cheese and 1/3 the bacon.

10. Repeat the above layer once more.

11. Place a tortilla. Spread remaining cheese and bacon.

12. Bake in a preheated oven at 350°F until the cheese melts and is golden brown at different spots.

Chicken 'n Waffles Casserole

Serves: 3-4

Ingredients:

- 5 toaster waffles

- 6 tablespoons milk

- 1 tablespoon melted butter

- Freshly ground black pepper to taste

- 3 eggs

- 2 tablespoons maple syrup + extra to drizzle

- Salt to taste

- 1 cup chopped breaded chicken

Method:

1. Place the waffles on a large baking sheet.

2. Bake in a preheated oven at 350°F for 7-10 minutes or until crisp.

3. Cool for a few minutes and chop into chunks. Place waffle chunks in a casserole dish. Add chicken and toss well.

4. Whisk together rest of the ingredients in a bowl and pour over the waffles and chicken.

5. Bake for 45 minutes or until the waffles are crisp.

6. Serve warm with a drizzle of maple syrup.

Loaded Cauliflower Breakfast Bake

Serves: 3

Ingredients:

- 1 medium head cauliflower, grated
- 5 large eggs
- 1 large clove garlic, minced
- Salt to taste
- 1 cup cheddar cheese
- Hot sauce to serve
- 4 slices bacon, chopped
- ½ cup whole milk
- 1 teaspoon paprika
- Freshly ground black pepper to taste
- 1 green onion, thinly sliced + extra to garnish

Method:

1. Place a skillet over medium heat. Add bacon. Cook until crisp. Remove bacon with a slotted spoon and place on a plate that is lined with paper towels.

2. Place cauliflower in a baking dish. Add eggs, garlic, milk, paprika, salt and pepper into a bowl and whisk well.

3. Spread bacon over the cauliflower. Sprinkle green onions.

4. Pour the egg mixture over the bacon.

5. Bake in a preheated oven at 350°F until golden brown.

Cheesy Hash Brown Casserole

Serves:

Ingredients:

- 12 eggs

- 9 slices bacon, chopped

- 3 tablespoons chopped chives

- 1 ½ cups cheddar cheese, shredded + extra to top

- 3 pounds frozen hash browns

- ¾ cup whole milk

- Freshly ground pepper to taste

- Salt to taste

Method:

1. Place a skillet over medium heat. Add bacon. Cook until crisp. Remove bacon with a slotted spoon and place on a plate that is lined with paper towels. Add hash browns and sauté for a couple of minutes.

2. Whisk together in a bowl egg and milk. Add hash browns and chives and stir.

3. Transfer half the mixture into a large baking dish.

4. Sprinkle half the cheese over it. Sprinkle ½ the bacon.

5. Repeat the above layer twice.

6. Bake in a preheated oven at 350°F until set.

Breakfast Casserole

Serves: 6

Ingredients:

- 1 ½ pounds ground breakfast sausage or ground meat

- 6 eggs beaten

- 5 scallions, chopped

- 5 turnips, peeled, grated

- Salt to taste

- Pepper powder to taste

Method:

1. Place a skillet over medium heat. Add sausages. Cook until brown. Break it simultaneously as it cooks. Turn off the heat.

2. Add eggs, scallions, turnips, salt and pepper. Mix well and transfer into a greased baking dish.

3. Bake in a preheated oven at 400 °F for 45 minutes. Cover the dish with foil and bake for another 25 minutes.

Chapter Three

Meatless Casserole Recipes

Classic Cheesy Mushroom and Broccoli Casserole

Serves: 3-4

Ingredients:

- 1 ½ tablespoons butter + extra to grease

- ¼ pound shiitake or baby Bella mushrooms, sliced

- 1 clove garlic, finely chopped

- 1 tablespoon all-purpose flour

- 2 tablespoons chopped onions

- ¼ teaspoon garlic powder

- ¾ cup heavy cream

- 5 ounces frozen chopped cauliflower, thawed, drained

- 1 ½ cups cooked rice

- ¼ teaspoon cayenne pepper

- ¼ cup stock

- 1 cup Cheddar – Monterey Cheese blend, shredded

- Salt to taste

- Pepper to taste

Method:

1. Grease a small casserole dish with a little butter.

2. Place a heavy bottomed skillet over medium heat. Add 1 ½ tablespoons butter and flour. Keep stirring until the color is golden brown.

3. Set aside ½ cup cheese and add rest of the ingredients and stir. Turn off the heat.

4. Transfer into the prepared casserole dish. Sprinkle cheese that was set aside.

5. Bake in a preheated oven at 425°F until the cheese melts and golden brown at different spots.

Classic Green Bean Casserole

Serves: 8-10

Ingredients:

- 2 cans cream of mushroom soup
- 2 teaspoons soy sauce
- 8 cups cut green beans, cooked
- 1 cup milk
- Pepper to taste
- 2 2/3 cups French fried onions

Method:

1. Set aside about 1 1/3 cup fried onions and add rest of the ingredients into a large casserole dish and stir.

2. Bake in a preheated oven at 350°F 30-40 minutes. Sprinkle the onions that were set aside.

3. Bake for another 5 minutes or until the onions turn golden brown.

Savory Tomato Cobbler

Serves: 3-4

Ingredients:

- 1 small sweet onion, chopped
- 1 medium tomato, chopped
- 1 ½ pounds assorted small tomatoes, divided
- 2 cloves garlic, minced
- ½ tablespoon olive oil
- ½ tablespoon champagne vinegar or white wine vinegar
- ½ teaspoon kosher salt
- ½ teaspoon fresh thyme leaves, chopped
- 1 tablespoon chopped chives
- 2 tablespoons fresh basil, chopped
- ¼ cup stone ground yellow cornmeal
- ¼ cup cold butter, cut into small pieces
- ½ cup + 2 tablespoons buttermilk
- ½ tablespoon cornstarch
- ¾ cup self-rising flour
- ¼ teaspoon baking powder
- 6 tablespoons Jarlsberg cheese, freshly shredded
- Freshly ground pepper to taste

Method:

1. Place a skillet over medium high heat. Add oil. When the oil is heated, add onions and sauté until translucent.

2. Stir in the chopped tomato, ¾ cup small tomatoes and garlic. Cook until soft.

3. Turn off the heat. Add cornstarch, salt, pepper and thyme leaves and stir.

4. Grease a baking dish. Spread remaining small tomatoes in the dish.

5. Spread the cooked tomatoes and stir gently.

6. Bake in a preheated oven at 375°F for 8-10 minutes.

7. Add flour, cornmeal and baking powder into a bowl. Add butter and cut with a pastry cutter until the mixture is crumbly. Cover and place in the refrigerator for 10 minutes.

8. Add cheese, basil and chives and mix well. Add buttermilk and stir until well combined.

9. Drop tablespoonsful of the mixture at different spots, taking care not to spread it.

10. Bake until golden brown. Cool for 30 minutes and then serve.

Broccoli Quinoa Casserole

Serves: 7-8

Ingredients:

- 3 ¼ cups quinoa, uncooked
- 3 cups fresh spinach
- 3 teaspoons cornstarch or arrowroot powder
- 5 green onions, chopped
- 3 cups fresh broccoli florets, steamed to tender crisp
- 6 ¾ cups low sodium vegetable stock or water
- Salt to taste 3 tablespoons pesto sauce
- 20 ounces skim mozzarella cheese, shredded
- ½ cup parmesan cheese, grated
- Pepper powder to taste
- 1/4 teaspoon red chili flakes

Method:

1. Add stock, pesto, cornstarch, pepper, chili flakes and salt into a bowl. Whisk well.

2. Transfer the mixture to a large saucepan. Place the saucepan over medium heat.

3. Turn off the heat when it begins to boil.

4. Meanwhile, place quinoa and green onions in a large baking dish. Pour the hot mixture over the quinoa. Layer with spinach, Parmesan and most of the mozzarella cheese. Cover the dish with foil.

5. Bake in a preheated oven at 400 °F for about 30 minutes.

6. Remove the dish from the oven. Add broccoli and stir well.

7. Cool slightly. Sprinkle rest of the mozzarella over it.

8. Uncover and bake for about 10 minutes.

Zucchini-and-Spinach Lasagna

Serves: 6

Ingredients:

- 1 ½ containers (8 ounces each) whipped chive and onion cream cheese

- ½ cup fresh basil, chopped + extra to garnish

- 3 ¼ pounds zucchini, thinly sliced

- 1 ½ packages (10 ounces each) fresh spinach

- 9 no boil lasagna noodles

- 1 ½ containers (15 ounces each) ricotta cheese

- 1 ½ teaspoons salt

- 3 tablespoons olive oil

- 3 cloves garlic, pressed

- 1 ½ packages (7 ounces each) shredded mozzarella cheese

Method:

1. Add cream cheese, ricotta cheese, salt and basil into a bowl and stir.

2. Place a large skillet over medium high heat. Add oil. When the oil is heated, add zucchini and sauté until light brown.

3. Add spinach and cook until it wilts. Add garlic and sauté until fragrant.

4. Transfer 1/3 of the vegetables into a large greased baking dish. Place 3 noodles.

5. Spread 1/3 of the ricotta mixture.

6. Repeat the above 2 layers twice. Sprinkle mozzarella cheese on top. Cover the dish with foil.

7. Bake in a preheated oven at 425°F 25-30 minutes. Uncover and bake for some more time until the cheese melts and golden brown at different spots.

8. Sprinkle some more basil on top and serve.

Vegan Shepherd's Pie

Serves: 3

Ingredients:

For mashed potatoes layer:

- 1 ½ pounds Yukon gold potatoes, thoroughly washed, halved

- 2 tablespoons vegan butter

- Salt to taste

- Pepper powder to taste

For the lentil layer:

- ¾ cup green or brown lentils, rinsed, soaked in water for 5-6 hours, drained

- 2 cups vegetable stock

- 1 small onion, chopped

- 1 clove garlic, minced

- 5 ounces bag mixed frozen vegetables

- ½ teaspoon dried thyme or 1 teaspoon fresh thyme, chopped

- ½ tablespoon olive oil

Method:

1. Add potatoes into a pot. Add salt and cover with water. Place the pot over medium heat.

2. When it begins to boil, lower heat and simmer until potatoes are cooked. Drain well and transfer into a bowl.

3. Mash with a potato masher until smooth. Add vegan butter, salt and pepper. Cover the bowl loosely and keep aside.

4. Grease a casserole dish with oil.

5. Place a saucepan over medium heat. Add oil. When the oil is heated, add onions and garlic and sauté until light golden brown. Add a bit of salt and pepper.

6. Add green lentils, vegetable stock, frozen vegetables, and thyme. When it begins to boil, lower heat and cover with a lid. Simmer until the lentils are tender.

7. Add vegetables, mix well, cover and cook for 10-15 minutes until nearly dry. Taste and adjust the salt and pepper. Transfer into the prepared dish. Spread it evenly.

8. Layer with the mashed potato layer.

9. Bake in a preheated oven at 425°F 25-30 minutes or until the mashed potatoes are slightly golden brown in color.

Fresh Vegetable Lasagna

Serves: 4

Ingredients:

- 2 medium zucchinis, halved lengthwise, thinly sliced
- 1 clove garlic, minced
- 1 small yellow bell pepper, chopped
- 1 small red bell pepper, chopped
- 1 onion, chopped
- 1 small egg
- ¾ cup fat free ricotta cheese
- 1 cup part skim mozzarella cheese, shredded, divided
- 4 ounces no boil lasagna noodles
- 4 ounces fresh mushrooms, sliced
- ¼ teaspoon salt or to taste
- 2 ½ cups basic marinara sauce
- Cooking spray
- ¼ cup parmesan cheese, freshly grated, divided

Method:

1. Grease a rimmed baking sheet with cooking spray. Place zucchini, garlic and mushrooms over the baking sheet.

2. Bake in a preheated oven at 450°F 12-14 minutes or until the vegetables are crisp as well as tender. Stir the vegetables half way through baking.

3. Remove these vegetables and place in a bowl.

4. Spread bell peppers and onions on the baking sheet. Bake for 10-12 minutes.

5. Lower the temperature of the oven to 350°F.

6. Add ricotta, ¾ cup mozzarella cheese, 2 tablespoons Parmesan cheese and egg into a bowl and mix well.

7. Grease a small baking dish with cooking spray. Pour about ½ cup marinara sauce in it. Spread it evenly.

8. Place 1 ½ - 2 noodles over it. Spread ½ cup sauce over the noodles followed by 1/3 the ricotta and 1/3 the vegetable mixture.

9. Repeat the above layer 2 more times.

10. Sprinkle remaining mozzarella cheese and Parmesan cheese on top. Cover the dish with foil.

11. Bake in a preheated oven at 350°F 30-40 minutes. Uncover and bake for a few more minutes until the cheese melts and is golden brown at different spots.

Chapter For

Slow Cooker Casserole Recipes

The same recipes can be also made in the oven. Follow the same procedure and layer the ingredients in a casserole dish. Place the dish in a preheated oven at about 350-425°F for 30-45 minutes.

Cheesy Chicken Tater Tot Casserole

Serves: 8-12

Ingredients:

- 2 pounds chicken breasts, boneless, skinless, chopped

- 2 bags (32 ounces each) frozen tater tots

- 4 cups cheddar cheese, shredded

- 6 ounces bacon, chopped

- Salt to taste

- Pepper to taste

- 1 ½ cups milk

- Nonstick cooking spray

Method:

1. Spray the inside of the slow cooker with cooking spray.

2. Place 1/3 the tater tots at the bottom of the pot. Layer with 1/3 the bacon followed by 1/3 cheese, chicken. Sprinkle salt and pepper on top.

3. Sprinkle 1/3 the bacon followed by 1/3 the cheese. Place remaining tater tots on top.

4. Sprinkle 1/3 the cheddar cheese and 1/3 the bacon. Pour milk all over.

5. Close the lid. Select 'Low' option and cook for 4-6 hours or on 'High' for 2-3 hours.

Enchilada Casserole

Serves: 8-9

Ingredients:

- 1 ½ pounds ground beef

- 1 ½ cans (10 ¾ ounces each) condensed cream of onion soup, undiluted

- 9 flour tortillas, torn

- 3 cans (10 ounces each) enchilada sauce

- ½ teaspoon salt or to taste

- 18 ounces cheddar cheese, shredded

Method:

1. Place a skillet over medium heat. Add beef. Sauté until the beef is not pink any more.

2. Remove beef with a slotted spoon and add into a bowl. Add enchilada sauce, salt and soup and stir.

3. Grease the inside of the slow cooker with cooking spray.

4. Spread 1/3 the beef mixture on the bottom of the pot. Spread 1/3 the tortillas followed by 1/3 the cheese.

5. Repeat the above layer 2 more times.

6. Close the lid. Select 'Low' option and cook for 4-6 hours or on 'High' for 2-3 hours.

Sweet Potato & Chicken Casserole

Serves: 4-6

Ingredients:

- 2 pounds chicken, skinless, boneless, chopped
- 10 ounces canned pineapple pieces, in juice
- 3 raw sweet potatoes, julienned
- 8 ounces chicken broth
- 1 tablespoon cornstarch mixed with 2 tablespoons water

Method:

1. Place chicken in the slow cooker. Layer with sweet potatoes followed by pineapple pieces along with juice.

2. Pour broth over the pineapple layer.

3. Close the lid. Select 'Low' option and cook for 4-6 hours or on 'High' for 2-3 hours.

4. Select 'High' option. Pour the cornstarch mixture and stir. Cook for a few minutes until the sauce becomes thick.

5. To serve: Place chicken and sweet potatoes on a serving platter. Pour the thickened sauce on top and serve.

Taco Casserole

Serves: 3

Ingredients:

- ¾ pound lean ground beef

- ½ can (from a 10.75 ounces can) condensed cream of onion soup

- 3 corn tortillas (6 inches each), cut into 1/2 inch strips

- ½ can (from a 14.5 ounces can) diced tomatoes with green chilies, with its liquid

- 0.5 ounce taco seasoning mix

- ¼ cup water

- ½ cup cheddar cheese, shredded

- 2 green onions, thinly sliced

- Salt to taste

- Pepper to taste

- ¼ cup sour cream

Method:

1. Place a skillet over medium heat. Add beef. Cook until brown. Break it simultaneously as it cooks.

2. Add beef, tomatoes, seasoning, and water into the slow cooker and stir.

3. Add tortilla strips and stir.

4. Close the lid. Select 'Low' option and cook for 7-8 hours or on 'High' for 3-4 hours.

5. Sprinkle cheese and onions. Top with sour cream and serve.

Broccoli, Brown Rice and Cheddar Casserole

Serves: 3

Ingredients:

- 1 tablespoon butter
- 2 tablespoons onions, finely chopped
- 1 tablespoon flour
- ½ cup low fat cheddar cheese, divided
- ¾ cup brown rice, uncooked
- 1 ¼ cup water
- ¼ cup mushrooms, finely chopped
- ½ pound broccoli florets, finely chopped
- 1 clove garlic, minced
- 1 cup milk
- ¼ cup walnuts, chopped (optional)
- 2 tablespoons parmesan cheese, grated
- Salt to taste
- Freshly ground pepper powder to taste

Method:

1. Place a saucepan over medium heat. Add butter. When butter melts, add onions, garlic, and mushrooms. Sauté until the onions are translucent.

2. Add salt, pepper and flour. Sauté until brown. Stir constantly.

69

3. Gently pour milk. Stir constantly and bring to a boil. Let it boil for a minute. Remove from heat.

4. Add half the cheese and mix well.

5. Add rice, water, broccoli, and cheese sauce into the slow cooker. Mix well.

6. Close the lid. Select 'Low' option and cook for 6 hours or on 'High' for 3 hours or until the rice is tender.

7. Uncover, sprinkle both cheddar cheese and Parmesan.

8. Cover and cook until cheese melts. Garnish with walnuts and serve.

Chapter Five

Dessert Casserole Recipes

Sweet Potato Dessert Casserole

Serves: 6-8

Ingredients:

- 7 Honey Maid Graham crackers, halved, divided

- ¼ cup packed brown sugar

- 1 ½ pounds sweet potatoes, baked, cooled

- 2 eggs, beaten

- 2 tablespoons butter, melted

- ¼ cup walnuts, chopped

- 7 ounces canned sweetened condensed milk

- 1 teaspoon pumpkin pie spice or to taste

Method:

1. Grease a square baking dish with cooking spray. Place half the graham pieces in a single layer in the baking dish.

2. Crush the remaining graham pieces and add into a bowl. Also add butter, sugar and walnuts. Mix until well combined.

3. Peel and mash the sweet potatoes in a bowl using a potato masher. Stir in the eggs, milk and pumpkin pie spice.

4. Spread this mixture over the grahams in the baking dish. Sprinkle the crushed graham mixture on top.

5. Bake in a preheated oven at 400°F for 10-15 minutes or until the top is golden brown.

6. Serve warm.

Pineapple Casserole Dessert

Serves: 7-8

Ingredients:

- ½ cup butter

- 3 eggs

- 4-5 slices bread, cut into cubes

- ¾ cup sugar

- 7.5 ounces canned crushed pineapple, drained

- 3 tablespoons cheddar cheese, shredded

Method:

1. Add butter and sugar into a mixing bowl. Beat with an electric mixer until smooth and creamy.

2. Add one egg at a time and beat well each time.

3. Add pineapple and bread crumbs and fold gently.

4. Grease a small baking dish with a little butter. Spoon the mixture into the dish. Spread it evenly.

5. Bake in a preheated oven at 325°F for about 45 minutes or until the dessert when pressed lightly, springs back.

6. Sprinkle cheese on top and bake for another 3-5 minutes.

7. Serve warm.

Banana Pudding

Serves: 4

Ingredients:

- 1 stick butter
- ½ teaspoon salt
- 6 ounces canned evaporated milk
- 3 egg yolks
- ½ bag vanilla wafers
- 1 cup sugar
- 6 tablespoons all-purpose flour
- 6 tablespoons milk
- ½ teaspoon vanilla extract
- 1 large banana, sliced

Method:

1. Set up a double boiler. Let the heat be set at medium low. Add butter into the heatproof bowl. When butter melts, add sugar, salt, milk, evaporated milk and flour. Using a whisk, whisk well.

2. Stir in the yolks and keep stirring until the mixture is thick. It may take about 30 minutes. Turn off the heat. Add vanilla extract and stir.

3. Place banana slices and wafers in a baking dish. Pour the thickened mixture over the banana slices.

4. Bake in a preheated oven at 325°F for about 20-25 minutes.

5. Cool completely and refrigerate until use.

Apple Bread Pudding with Vanilla Sauce

Serves: 4

Ingredients:

For pudding:

- 2 cups soft bread, cut into cubes
- 1 egg, beaten
- 2 tablespoons raisins
- ½ teaspoon vanilla extract
- ½ cup brown sugar
- 1 1/3 cups milk
- 1 tablespoon butter or margarine
- 1 cup apples, peeled, cored, thinly sliced
- ½ teaspoon ground cinnamon

For vanilla sauce:

- 2 tablespoons brown sugar
- 2 tablespoons white sugar
- ¼ cup milk
- ¼ cup butter or margarine
- ½ teaspoon vanilla extract

Method:

1. To make pudding: Place a skillet over medium heat. Add butter. When butter melts, add pecans, raisins and apple. Cook for a few minutes until the apple is

tender. Turn off the heat. Carefully remove the butter from the skillet and add into a baking dish. Grease the dish with this butter.

2. Place bread in a bowl. Add the apple mixture into it and mix gently. Set aside for a while.

3. Place a saucepan over medium heat. Add brown sugar, milk and butter. Stir until butter melts and sugar just dissolves. Do not heat for long.

4. Whisk together eggs, vanilla extract and cinnamon. Add into the milk mixture. Mix well. Pour this over the bread.

5. Bake in a preheated oven at 350°F for about 30-45 minutes or until set.

6. Meanwhile, make the vanilla sauce as follows: Add all the ingredients except vanilla to a saucepan and bring to a boil.

7. Turn off the heat and add vanilla. Pour over the pudding and serve.

Conclusion

Thank you for purchasing the book.

As a child, you may have had more casseroles than you can remember. These dishes were the easiest to make and the smell made you feel at ease no matter how you were feeling. If you had a bad day, all you needed was a plate of mom's casserole. Well, if you are not familiar with how to make them, this book has taken you through that.

The recipes in the book cover the simplest and classic casserole recipes that have clear instructions that will help you make the best casserole. If someone is coming over to visit, there is a new addition to the family, or you have had a bad day at work, whip up a casserole. If you lead a busy life, whip up a casserole over the weekend and split the dish to cover one of your meals for every day of the week.

I hope you enjoy the recipes in the book. Happy cooking!

Thank you and good luck!

Other Books by Grizzly Publishing

Panini Press Cookbook: Delicious Panini Recipes From Around The World

https://www.amazon.com/dp/B07CRBV85Y

Cheesecake Cookbook: Delicious Cheesecake Recipes From Around The World

https://www.amazon.com/dp/B079TZ4ZDZ

Brazilian Instant Pot Cookbook: Delicious Pressure Cooked Meals Made Fast and Easy

https://www.amazon.com/dp/B078XBYP89

Norwegian Cookbook: Traditional Scandinavian Recipes Made Easy

https://www.amazon.com/dp/B079M2W223

Russian Cookbook: Traditional Russian Recipes Made Easy

https://www.amazon.com/dp/B079LYXJKF

CPSIA information can be obtained
at www.ICGtesting.com
Printed in the USA
BVHW042017280321
603523BV00028B/735

9 781952 395703